YOUR IMMACULATE HEART

Your Immaculate Heart

Poems by Annmarie O'Connell

Copyright © Annmarie O'Connell 2016

No part of this book may be used or performed without written consent from the author, if living, except for critical articles or reviews.

O'Connell, Annmarie
1st edition.

ISBN: 978-0-9855292-9-1
Library of Congress Control Number: 2014954705

Interior Layout by Lea C. Deschenes
Cover Design by Dorinda Wegener
Cover Photo by H. Steven Lawley
Editing by Matt Mauch and Tayve Neese

Printed in Tennessee, USA
Trio House Press, Inc.
Ponte Vedra Beach, FL

To contact the author, send an email to tayveneese@comcast.net

Rocky and Waylon Kostyk this one is for you.

Your Immaculate Heart

I.
MEN

3	Man Sitting By the Roadside
4	The Old Man Who Knew Me 10 Years Ago
5	When the Wind Ripples Through the Trees
6	The Man Who Lives In the Abandoned Garage
7	The Man Who Lives Without Angels
8	The Men Spill Out of the Factory
9	In the Vacant Lot
10	At Dusk, People Are In a Hurry
11	Each Day His Empty Chair Sits in the Simple Kitchen
12	I Met a Man Who Does Not See
13	The Black-Mustached Man and His Disabled Daughter Are Relatives
14	It Is Noon
15	One Day In November
16	A Single Bird Waits On the Empty Clothesline
17	Some Days I Think of That Man Who Doesn't Like Me
18	When the Cashier Unexpectedly Asks You

19	The Old Man Trips Up the Step
20	The Retired Cop Turned Mechanic

II.
BOYS

23	Having Lived In a Ruined World
24	It Makes Sense to Let You Wear Your Little Gym Shoes Through the Living Room Now
25	When You Lean Your Head On My Back
26	A Shaft of Sunlight Enters the Earth
27	You Seem to Have Everything
28	The Boy Drags His Doll
29	Right Before the Lightning Storm
30	The Polish Teenager
31	You See the Spiny Claws of a Tree

III.
HISTORY

35	Everything Is True In The Other Life
36	The First Afternoon After That Day
37	Look How Everyone Finds Happiness

38	My Grandfather Carried a Brown Case
39	The Thing About You Is
40	The Man In the Blue Uniform
41	Tonight One Half of You
42	Just Because There Are Beatings
43	Your Father Is the Bully
44	When Your Father Bends Over

IV.
DESTINY

47	In the Waiting Room
48	Solemn, Wide-Mouthed Streets
49	This Morning's Light
50	I Bring 73 Year Old Mary Food
51	The Waitress Who Lives In the Red-White
52	That Woman Riding the Bus East-Bound on 55th Street
53	When the Cashier Tries to Steal My $7
54	Compared to the Sweet Lilacs
55	Another Year Has Gone
56	The Angels On Their Porches
57	Like Drizzle
58	In the End
59	Admit How Gently the World

I.
MEN

Man Sitting By the Roadside

Deliver us from breathing time into open fists.
From wasting just enough to fill this gray jar with forever.

Man sitting by the roadside,
deliver us from wanting too much
love or something else
with your name written all over it.

Man sitting by the roadside,
surrender your hungry gaze,
let it roll down our faces and bodies
and echo back to feed you
on your feet.

Man sitting by the roadside,
deliver us from evil
over and over again.

The Old Man Who Knew Me 10 Years Ago

does not recognize me at the grocery store.
He spends his time fixing things.
He walks the long night
hunting for her years on earth,
scaring himself into thinking of her face.

Occasionally, he recalls the last place they touched,
how he drew small streams into her delicate palms.

Every hour he regrets
not placing his head on her shoulder,
burning it into the shape of twenty four stars.

I shudder at how small we are.
Up to our knees in loneliness.

When the Wind Ripples Through the Trees

the man lying in his living
room hospital bed
leans just out of reach
like he's feeling his way in the dark—

the holy strangeness of lavender and violet
looping across his window.

Every so often,
the sun streams through the vertical blinds,
his long body stretches out—
the brilliant warmth
trickles through him.

Suddenly you long for
the faces you love
their delicate bodies
blessed inch by inch.

The Man Who Lives In the Abandoned Garage

touches the baby's cheek with his dirtiest hand.
With the other, he gives him a handful of grass.

He stares into the ground
like he's searching for faces in the surface of water.

The baby brings a single green-yellow blade to his lips.
The rest slip through his little fingers.

The Man Who Lives Without Angels

hurriedly carries the young boy across 63rd street
and into the clinic.

At the same exact time as my sorrow,
a pure amber storm folds us over
then slowly tumbles across our bodies.

Disappointment brings tattered
things directly into light,
so we can feel the fallen
blossoms under our feet.

I think of you lying in the hospital,
stitched up and staring at the sides of buildings.
The flowers wither by the plastic Virgin Mary statue
you needed by your side.

I think of the woman tipping your chin,
and how at just the right angle
she can see drops of sea
in the folds of your eyes.

The woman gives up
a piece of her own body to lift yours.

For every man tossed into a deep rooted grave,
two more get carried.

The Men Spill
Out of the Factory

in a cloud of smoke
in the same direction
where I sit waiting
to give my house
to the bank. How strange it is to be the hungry animal
between their teeth and the world
was warm milk all along.

Past the telephone pole
and the white gym shoes
strung over it,
past FOR SALE signs,
past that little girl
sulking on the curb,

the happy sheriff sits in a crowded
restaurant on a phone call to his mother.
She paces the kitchen in & out
of sadness with the cord
between her blue-gray
fingers, unable to speak of her own fear
of death, unable to speak of the loneliness
flinging itself around
the dark house,
in this old parting place
she is a child
gone missing—
looking for new things
to hold.

In the Vacant Lot

The men who wake up thirsty
huddle together in the last ray
slowly cascading off their cold bodies.

You can understand how the sound of a train bulldozing by in the
distance burns like 1000 suns in their iron sides.

You cannot understand how the sound of a man's own jagged
tongue breaks him open wide.

At Dusk, People Are In a Hurry

Some have dreams that slither into the dark
behind their eyes.

I wait at a cold bus stop
with an old man,
his two hands touching
a VFW hat that salutes
the harsh wind.

Out of nowhere
I want to smear love
into the grooves of his palm.

Sometimes you can see the light
turn on in things that are alive.

Each Day His Empty Chair Sits in the Simple Kitchen

and sheds a dream so clear
she can almost see him tumble out of the ragged seat.
His long spine barking at the world
in agony over the air we're breathing.

The great distances he went
to abandon
the happiness growing inside him.

Now here he is by the cold window,
born again for nothing.

I Met a Man Who Does Not See

the green leaves dropping from the trees.
He wanders through his front room,
the adjacent walls and the picture of the beautiful woman
still warm in a casket in the cold ground
stir to life at the tip of his fingers.

He stands in front of me on the littered sidewalk,
squinting through wind that slightly moves his gracious body
into the busy street.

Even with the tremendous world
motionless and over us,
we spend all our lives learning
to be brave.

The Black-Mustached Man and His Disabled Daughter Are Relatives

you haven't met yet. A tree with bare claws for hands tells you to listen to all their singing back and forth. She walks along the edge of the park by the swings and they sway back and forth from the wind. Empty swinging. Because she's some relative you already love her. Her familiar singing. Her hands an accomplice to her face. Familiar pairing of hands and cheeks. Things you already love. A tree tells you to listen to that tired wife tearing a plastic bag open with her teeth. Familiar teeth. Today you believe in familiar trees and faces. Now you owe them everything.

It Is Noon

A man clatters down
your alley. He stops to stare at the flock
of birds that surprised you
with their meeting in a dead bush.
He stares at you with his head to the side
and imagines he knows you. He wants to whisper
in your ear about how he becomes
terrible. He wants you to tell him
that once in awhile
he's not that broken.
His slender body becomes more distant
and you suddenly want to extend your hand
over that silver gate and say something like:
As a matter of fact, I love you also.
Instead you stare down the dirty alley,
baffled in both directions.

One Day In November

when the city is still, quiet
you go to the post office and wait in line
with your insignificant body
for the man who cannot hear working behind the counter.

He listens to your desperate face as you write down
a zip code on a tiny piece of paper and place it in his hand.
He suddenly reminds you of a dream
where you dared to let go
of the walls you were holding together.

If you can at least get him to feel
it's still beautiful to be visible,
you may sing the world open
all the way home.

A Single Bird Waits On the Empty Clothesline

feverishly shaking the rain off his wings.
You sit in the park and wait
for the sound of the baby
girl's laughter in between the wind
after the man pretends to kick her
as she comes swinging down from
the sky.

After you hear it,
a man from across the street tosses
his bag of garbage out the car window

and it lands in someone's front yard.
He waits for his father to hug him,
or at least touch him, like that dog
waits there by the young boy as he waves
a stick in front of his mouth. The drool runs down
his furry throat. His teeth clench
and miss. He's only a whimper
or two away.

Some Days I Think of That Man Who Doesn't Like Me

on his hands and knees, bent over his toilet
trying to scrub it clean. I don't care what they told you,
we are enormous when we're dead; a million
pelts of grass blowing west, together,
throwing mountains off center
one by one.

When the Cashier Unexpectedly Asks You

about the day you die,
his heart almost visible
like the trunk of the tree
in the long window,
you think of the man asleep
and hiding in the bushes across the street.

A person will always be talking or humming
or getting tossed aside.
Someone will always be born empty-handed
into the dark of a hollow net.

My body is here but not for long.
The hours fly past me as I sit on the bench
next to the woman who talks so sweetly to something in her
    deep purple bag.

You want to tell him
that at the exact moment of death,
we're navigating weeds.

The Old Man Trips Up the Step

and his glasses fall onto the pavement.
You get on your knees
before the church doors,
your head slightly bent
to pick them up.

He tells you we are more beautiful
than all the grains of sand on the earth,

this clumsy angel blown from the sky,
blown over the row on row of houses,
right into your immaculate heart.

As if he lies with you in your bed
crying in the dark. As if you just realized
you waste your little life.

The Retired Cop Turned Mechanic

comes in from your alley whispering,
Tessa Tessa Tessa.
The little rat darts away from his feet
like a quiet slant of rain.
In the shadows, two single yellow flowers
stand away from each other, separated
by a shower cap that blew in from the busy street.
The blinking Currency Exchange sign
peeks over your garage.
Someone's wind chime
sings to you. A loose strumming at the end
of your night. The night
isn't over yet.

II.
BOYS

Having Lived In a Ruined World

It's nice to have a restless body
flutter past the shaking window,
his little arms the shape of wings.

It Makes Sense to Let You Wear Your Little Gym Shoes Through the Living Room Now

Before you're sprung forth into the cracks. Before the city rolls over you and gets lodged in the bend of your elbow. For now, I keep the green leafy things out of your mouth. I walk and climb with you in baby-leg galaxies. I rinse you out with all my might. As poor as you have been, you can still command grace. For us there's a wintering tree on every corner. When you spend the whole night spinning out like a gutted machine, I will love you enough to stitch you up alive.

When You Lean Your Head On My Back

I remember how you stepped
into the world early,
shouting

It is not lonely

dragging us off our knees.

(the bright red blur
inside the lick of a flame)

A Shaft of Sunlight Enters the Earth

The way death enters us
so miraculously inside.
That is the moment everything stops.
When even things that decay remind me of his sweetness.

The baby asleep beside me will exist
after I have fallen off the earth.
In the middle of it all,
that moment he goes
so completely inside himself,
he will look up into

a thousand streaks of dead
lighting up the sky, the mightiest of stars.

You Seem to Have Everything

until the young boy at the disheveled park
strides toward you and the place you rest your dark eyes.
He stomps after his mother in mighty bursts.
He calls her name into the folds of his dirty palms for the rest of
his life.

You can feel
the rhythmic pounding of every foot-
step zap your sluggish brain,
lick it clean as a bone.

The Boy Drags His Doll

to the edge of a field
and abandons it.

Stay here

his heart turning
into whispers
for mile after mile.

Right Before
the Lightning Storm

The baby runs away from the woman
with too much weariness behind
the pupils of her eyes.

Listen to the shrieking laughter
between the crashing winds.
How it stops the whole
reeling world.

The Polish Teenager

working behind the deli counter,
the one with *thug life* tattooed
on his skinny neck,
happened to you.

Today
seemed so good
something's taking shape
in you,
alive and whatever it is that seemed
to have died inside you
is now worn on the outside of your body
where you stand in the middle of the corner store
clutching a package of meat
like your life
depends on it.

You See the Spiny Claws of a Tree

and it's so much uglier
than the half leaning tree next to it,
half-covered in yellow-orange burnt leaves
which seem to wave at you.
You want to know if it's okay
to wonder about the way things weather.
Your body disappears into a flurry of leaves
that confuse you in the warmth,
like how beautiful the little
boy looks standing there in front
of the black diamond city-
linked fence by the filthy railroad tracks.
You want to show him
the things you're afraid to leave behind.

III.
HISTORY

Everything Is True
In The Other Life

so do not ridicule the man
hovering over himself,
crying into a box of old socks.

Sooner or later
you will have to apologize
for those mountains.

The First Afternoon After That Day

you can no longer differentiate me
from the pile of dirt
that feeds the pale green
string of city trees,
you will pull down the blinds
above the bed—
crush the pieces of sunlight
wanting in.

You will get on the bus and tell the mother
who wipes the corners of her baby's mouth
something about the hardest part
of beginning again.

I will be the passing shadow
across your knees
loving you into night.

Look How Everyone Finds Happiness

one room at a time,
like night isn't rushing into
your bedroom where you stand weeping
at the sight of your own body.

Outside the windows,
your children carry little statues
in their pockets, just so they can bury
and crush them with their heels.

Don't forget your mother
is still dying and everything
is at or around your feet.

My Grandfather Carried a Brown Case

swatting and dodging thugs
and their baseball bats while he made his way
to work at the factory.

I often wondered how they couldn't
take to his flesh or know how
to wait for a word in the mouth
when he opened it and tried to yell out
in broken English: *Someone will save me.*
To put it another way
what would the world be
if something caught fire in every shaky heart
in every chop shop
in every alley
across the city.

Go ahead and try to beat the faith
out of a man—

the graceful way
he never begins to live
a life.

The Thing About You Is

you're as temporary as that drunk man stumbling
toward you on the street so go ahead and look
him dead in the eye like he's your brother
with the thousand yard stare sulking at the dinner table.

Bend yourself to shake him up—
something loud and true.
Don't act like you don't mean it.

The Man In the Blue Uniform

Does what must be done, even to us
or those lucky enough
to be brought home to fall apart.

The baby bird lies in the entrance way to the park,
fighting—it just won't hold still.
The man sweeps up the little body
into a filthy dustpan and that is that.

Birds of another world
are not afraid to mend.
Birds of another world teach the other birds how to weep
in song and own the crystal air.

They don't get how,
even on a quiet little afternoon,
we carry a nest in our arms
and beg for one more miracle.

Tonight One Half of You

rides the subway with that skinny version
of your mother who sits there smiling
into a brown paper bag.

I won't look down on you
if you get off three stops too soon
with no regrets.
Count yourself lucky.
Spill into what is left of the city
the pulsing street—
a spur of light—
then spend the whole night
cradling your future life.

Just Because There Are Beatings

and death and things burning away
right in front of your eyes, or a body
floating and eating away at that sand
castle on some shore, doesn't mean the sun
cannot press itself into your sister's
yellow hair while she frantically brushes it
or the rain cannot drip out of the gutter
and into a man's mouth where he sits
on the concrete smiling and yelling at you.

Your Father Is the Bully

sitting on the park bench
who can't afford to buy you
a new pair of shoes
or a haircut.

It is the first day of real spring
and you're sitting
in the dirt on the ground
afraid to touch it.

The woman walks over to where you sit
to hand you a ball
and you find yourself
tossing it higher and higher
into the air
until it becomes a tiny blue speck
against the giant new sun
that seems to shine on absolutely nothing
but you.

When Your Father Bends Over

the trunk of his 1981 Buick in the alley of your house
every Wednesday and hands the homeless man with the blue-knit
hat a black garbage bag filled with aluminum cans,
you remember the fact that we're all going to die.

You can't say
you never saw two angels
scraping at the roundness of the world
in silence and out of the way.

IV.
DESTINY

In the Waiting Room

the man pulls his crying wife
closer to him and she rests
her head on his shoulder.
Outside there is no place to be still.
Two tall weeds poke through the metal fence.
A tiny plane floats through the clouds.
The blonde boy tumbles
over the yellow truck,
and on the top of the bare tree,
a black plastic bag flutters on
a branch, everything barely
holding on in the wind.

Solemn, Wide-Mouthed Streets

Wear a betrayed look.
When they're ravaged,
miserable people bury fistfuls of every loss.
Sweaty, unclenched palms work the familiar
dirt beds.

We drift
with dull melodies of weeks turning
over and over—a ringing
in our ears.

It's like this:

even when we can't see it,
we stretch over ourselves
to reach for a small piece
of the floating world.

This Morning's Light

gives you a certain gentleness
over the long slope of your nose.

The milky sky,
so bent on listening
to the quick of your breath.
So bent on witnessing
the reel of our lives,
like it plucked them out
of itself somehow.

A dark-pink landscape drips
over the edges of our half-open door.
through the thick crack,
little arms dangle–
reach out to bless us all.

I Bring 73 Year Old Mary Food

she looks at me and then my son
like we're tiny broken elements
stuck in a kaleidoscope.
Her lungs rattle the room,
whirring beats of years
leaving bodies.

Mary never forgets to tell me about her 6 out-of-state children.
My son is dead, as if right then the earth would sprout and give us
his face—rich, blue eyes, typical for blessing the living.

All I have to offer today is news:
a single Bleeding Heart grows effortlessly alone
in her backyard garden.

The Waitress Who Lives In the Red-White

brick bungalow across the street
will be dead in 10 years.

Right now, she's making little gestures
and fixing the American flag permanently
posted on her front porch.
Right now, she is whispering a song
and eyeing her ashy skin.
Right now, she is walking with the back of her palms
on her wine-bottle hips.
She yells her son in from the streets.

The liquid sundown insists
it wants no part in this.

That Woman Riding the Bus East-Bound on 55th Street

should've left that man 30 years ago. Doesn't mean she can't
tell you to fumble around for that dream you had.
Never mind that. Sit yourself closer and watch a life
try to gnaw its way out of her. Going in the same exact direction
as people you've never met makes everything feel like its slipping
out of reach. Stop being everyone's accuser. Remember her face.
You will look for it in the rubble.

When the Cashier Tries to Steal My $7

I don't shout or mourn or think
of her father bending over a double stroller
saying: *Boys? You got lucky two times.*

So what's it to you
if I kneel in the street
and listen to her heartbeat
churning the city
to sleep?

I pretend like
she doesn't owe me
a thing.

Compared to the Sweet Lilacs

we're burnt out stars.

Still, I wonder what stops you
from leaping into the arms
of the stuttering man on the street,
his body a distant shadow
there is no trace of.
An eyelash of a wish peeks out
the two slits of his eyes.

Now I'm going to tell you to kiss his narrow mouth.
Now I'm going to tell you to bind us to the shivering marvel
in the road.

Another Year Has Gone

and digs itself silently into various
parts of your body
but you make it to the market
anyway.

You wait in line
and just like that
you think of your last solitary
cry and hope to God
it thins out like a thread
then settles into the dark
of the bucket of azaleas
that old man
bends over to see.

The Angels On Their Porches

The angel elbows on the spiny rails
The angels sitting in a pillow of smoke
The angels lying on one another in the light
The angels spit out by a gust of wind
The angels falling into the past
The angels chewing on the wet black of the earth
The heavy rumble of angels
wading through the pink blossoms
The heavy rumble of dreams
inside angels

Like Drizzle

we're so delicate and happening
now. The next person you touch—
more fragile than glass,
more alive than the small woman
sitting at the kitchen table
around the gray tile
rubbing the back of her son's
neck, running her fingers through
his dark black hair.

In the End

The toothless woman
who apologetically stares at my pregnant belly
with a cigarette dangling from her lips
will let you in
without wasting time
shout your name on the street
just to say hello
notice when you're a pile
of torn bits
offer you her last
cup of light
tell you the honest to God truth
about breaking apart

Admit How Gently the World

touches you. Put that old man to sleep
wrestling inside you. You never know
what your children will become
or for that matter who the hell
is knocking on your car window.

This is your grain of sand.
This is your drop of water.
This is your place on earth
and when it's gone
it floats.

Acknowledgments

I am grateful to the following magazines in which some of these poems first appeared:

A-Minor Magazine ("You See the Spiny Claws of a Tree," "You Seem to Have Everything," "The First Afternoon After The Day"); *Thrush* ("It Makes Sense To Let You Wear Your Little Gym Shoes In the Living Room Now"); *SOFTBLOW* ("At Dusk, People Are In a Hurry," "When The Wind Ripples Through the Trees," "When the Cashier Unexpectedly Asks You," "The Man Who Lives Without Angels"); *Right Hand Pointing* ("Having Lived In a Ruined World"); *The Rusty Nail* ("Solemn, Wide-Mouthed Streets"); *Whiskey Island Magazine* ("Compared to the Sweet Lilacs"); *The 2River View* ("A Single Bird Waits On the Empty Clothesline"); *Curbside Splendor Publishing E-Zine* ("My Grandfather Carried a Brown Case"); *Escape Into Life* ("The Polish Teenager," "Look How Everyone Finds Happiness," "That Woman Riding the Bus East-Bound on 55th Street"); *Anthem Journal* ("Tonight One Half of You," "That Black- Mustached Man and His Disabled Daughter Are Relatives")

These poems also appeared in *Her Last Cup of Light,* a chapbook published by Aldrich Press in 2013: "I Bring 73 Year Old Mary Food," "This Morning's Light," "When You Lean Your Head On My Back," "A Shaft of Sunlight Enters the Earth," "Man Sitting By the Roadside," "The Boy Drags His Doll," "The Man In the Blue Uniform," "The Man Who Lives In the Abandoned Garage," "Right Before the Lightning Storm," "In the Vacant Lot," "The Waitress Who Lives In the Red-White," "Each day His Empty Chair Sits in the Simple Kitchen," and "I Met a Man Who Does Not See."

A sincerest thank you to Matt Mauch and the rest of Trio House Press for believing in my work.

Thank you to Lauren Gordon for her constant support and so many edits.

About the Author

Annmarie O'Connell is the author of two chapbooks, *Eleanor* (Dancing Girl Press) and *Her Last Cup of Light* (Aldrich Press). Her poetry has appeared or is forthcoming with *Verse Daily, Slipstream, SOFTBLOW, THRUSH Poetry Journal, Vinyl Poetry, 2River View,* and *Anthem Journal,* along with several other journals and magazines. She is a lifelong resident of the South side of Chicago.

About the Artist

H. Steven Lawley is a psychotherapist and soccer coach in Colorado. He takes photos on the side.

About the Book

Your Immaculate Heart was designed at Trio House Press
through the collaboration of:

Matt Mauch, Lead Editor
Tayve Neese, Supporting Editor
H. Steven Lawley, Cover Photo
Dorinda Wegener, Cover Design
Lea Deschenes, Interior Design

The text is set in Adobe Caslon Pro.

The publication of this book is made possible, whole or in part,
by the generous support of the following individuals and/or agencies:

Anonymous

About the Press

Trio House Press is a collective press. Individuals within our organization come together and are motivated by the primary shared goal of publishing distinct American voices in poetry. All THP published poets must agree to serve as Collective Members of the Trio House Press for twenty-four months after publication in order to assist with the press and bring more Trio books into print. Award winners and published poets must serve on one of four committees: Production and Design, Distribution and Sales, Educational Development, or Fundraising and Marketing. Our Collective Members reside in cities from New York to San Francisco.

Trio House Press adheres to and supports all ethical standards and guidelines outlined by the CLMP.

Trio House Press, Inc. is dedicated to the promotion of poetry as literary art, which enhances the human experience and its culture. We contribute in an innovative and distinct way to American Poetry by publishing emerging and established poets, providing educational materials, and fostering the artistic process of writing poetry. For further information, or to consider making a donation to Trio House Press, please visit us online at: www.triohousepress.org.

Other Trio House Press Books you might enjoy:

Bone Music by by Stephen Cramer
    2015 Louise Bogan Award selected by Kimiko Hahn

*Rigging a Chevy into a Time Machine and Other Ways
    to Escape a Plague* by Carolyn Hembree
    2015 Trio Award Winner selected by Neil Shepard

Magpies in the Valley of Oleanders by Kyle McCord, 2015

The Alchemy of My Mortal Form by Sandy Longhorn
    2014 Louise Bogan Winner selected by Carol Frost

What the Night Numbered by Bradford Tice
    2014 Trio Award Winner selected by Peter Campion

Flight of August by Lawrence Eby
    2013 Louise Bogan Winner selected by Joan Houlihan

The Consolations by John W. Evans
    2013 Trio Award Winner selected by Mihaela Moscaliuc

Fellow Odd Fellow by Steven Riel, 2013

Clay by David Groff
    2012 Louise Bogan Winner selected by Michael Waters

Gold Passage by Iris Jamahl Dunkle
    2012 Trio Award Winner selected by Ross Gay

If You're Lucky Is a Theory of Mine by Matt Mauch, 2012

www.ingramcontent.com/pod-product-compliance
Lightning Source LLC
Chambersburg PA
CBHW030604020526
44112CB00048B/1224